Andy

BY CHRISTOPHER MAKOS

© 2001 Assouline Publishing, Inc.

Assouline Publishing, Inc.
601 West 26ᵗʰ Street
18ᵗʰ floor
New York, NY 10001
USA
www.assouline.com

Introduction: Courtesy Ingrid Sischy. *Interview* magazine / Brant Publications ©.
This text originally appeared in the April 1996 issue of *Interview*.

ISBN: 2 84323 279 1

Printed in Italy.

Andy

BY CHRISTOPHER MAKOS

ASSOULINE

Andy Mania

by Ingrid Sischy

Andy Warhol may have become a household name as he wanted to, he may have appeared on the TV show *The Love Boat*, and he may have hobnobbed with the fancy folk as well as being a lightning rod for the underground. He may have made movies and written books, he may have been the force behind the magazine *Interview,* but first and foremost, he was an artist. It was all part of his art. Warhol was an artist who changed American culture. It will never look the same now that we have seen it through his eyes. Part of what he did was to re-present it in a way that seemed true and real to him. This is the point of art—to capture things as they are in their essence, and also to describe the world. Warhol described America in particular—and the paintbrush was just one of the tools with which he captured and changed our culture.

Despite Warhol's apparent infatuation with power and with fame, his attraction was never something that treated power and fame as though it were above society. It was all part of the mix of how he recorded contemporary life, and if you look at his paintings, you'll see that it all got the same dead-on look that he brought to all his subjects. You'll also see that a lot of the time his art evened things out.

Warhol was always an observer, which means he never lost what an artist is—the one who can see what others might miss. He was probably such a consummate observer because he was a consummate outsider. Don't be fooled by the fact that you're always seeing pictures of him that make it look like he was a part of so many in-crowds. In fact, the power of those pictures is that they show Warhol breaking down the boundaries that usually surround things. I've always thought that in one way or another Warhol was always in a kind of drag. To some he was a clown, to some he was a weirdo, to some he was a great date for a fancy soiree, to some he was just the artist to invite to a White House "do", to some he was just the social portraitist that would immortalize them, to some he was the leader of the gang, to some he was a guy who said he wanted to be like a machine, to others he was that strange fellow in a wig, et cetera. He was like a chameleon who could move from circumstance to circumstance and always fit in, but still be himself. This is how he went in and out of so many worlds, and ended up capturing so many of them for us to have on record now he is gone. Even in his lifetime, to many people Warhol was the greatest American artist. He never acted that way though. He was never all puffed up about being great. He took the opposite approach—the "I don't have a good idea, do you?" approach. This doesn't prove that he wasn't creative, but that he was a good editor as well as a brilliant observer. To be a certain kind of great artist you have to be a sharp editor, you have to be able to recognize the stuff that gets to the heart of things. You have to admit the role that others have in what you do, whether they're others from the past or the present. Warhol was interested in both. The same part of him that made him a great editor is what made him an insatiable collector. The value of something isn't what would turn him on as a collector. His obsession for instance with inexpensive cookie jars is now legendary. Of course he liked the fact that they became valuable, but it was the way they reminded him of his childhood that grabbed him in the first place. People like to say that he was cynical, but the people who knew him well always talk about his childlike innocence. In a way you have to have that innocence, as well as that knowingness about human nature that he had, if you're going to be an artist. Because you have to be able to see things freshly. He did and that is why he was often able to capture things in a way that they hadn't been seen before. Warhol's capacity for innocence is also why he could have an excitement for new things and new people. He didn't get all satisfied with his circumstances as a famous artist and stop wanting to know what was going on. He understood that if he did this, he'd stop being able to do his work. Unlike many people who make it big, he didn't look down his nose at the next generations to come along. In fact, he wanted to be among the new artists who interested him, and who maybe made him feel competitive. This kind of meta-engagement is what engages people so much about him today. He was ageless, boundaryless, and that's why what he did will probably be of interest forever, even though so much of it appears to be so simple. It hit our culture on the nose.

Interview April 1996

Andy

by Christopher Makos

Andy Warhol and I first talked about collaborating on a photo project in late 1980. I was immediately excited by the idea and knew I wanted to do it. But I wanted to make sure we were going to create something new and different, rather than simply trade on his celebrity. He had already been photographed by many famous photographers, including Irving Penn and Horst.

Not that I was any slouch; the reason I attracted Andy's interest (other than my blonde hair and youthful, boundless energy) was because of the success I had already achieved. This great artist loved success of any kind, and he liked successful young men most of all. In 1977, I had published a collection of photographs titled *White Trash,* which had attracted a lot of attention. *White Trash* included mavens of contemporary culture—Tennessee Williams, Halston, Marilyn Chambers (the Ivory soap spokeswoman turned porn star), Liza Minnelli, John Lennon, Paul Getty and others—along with pictures of the emerging punk rock music scene, with Debbie Harry (Blondie), Richard Hell and Robert Mapplethorpe's favorite, Patti Smith.

The visual juxtaposition of celebrity culture with an emerging downtown punk culture that had not yet found understanding among the masses was a first, and a source of endless fascination to him. He didn't just love the images themselves, he loved the whole book—the spirit, the photographic style, the art direction and the people in it. Andy actually bought 1,000 *White Trash* books for his time capsules. He asked me to sign every one of them, and of course, learning from him, I told him it would cost one dollar a signature. He understood, as this was the philosophy that he had taught me: "Art is money, and money is art."

In 1979, Andy asked me to art direct his first photography book, *Exposures*. That book documented the rich and famous, not-so-rich and not-so-famous, the barely clothed, fashion moguls, society matrons, artists and other eccentrics that passed before his small Minox camera that only he thought was a secret.

Andy loved my work (he called me "the most modern photographer in America") and he loved carrying a camera, which he did from the late 1970s, when we became close friends, until he died in 1987. I learned a lot from him and he learned from me, particularly about photography. Ours was a creative collaboration in the truest sense, with an ever-flowing exchange of ideas, inspiration and technical knowledge.

In addition to printing the photographs for *Exposures,* my studio also printed his "sewn photographs," which I art directed. These pictures were exhibited at the Robert Miller Gallery on 57th Street. The idea for the sewn photograph came from when I was a child, growing up in Lowell, Massachusetts. My mother had a sewing machine, and I used to amuse myself by sewing pieces of paper together. I suggested the idea to Andy as a way to sell multiples of his photos and he liked it.

I art directed the sewn photographs with rough edges, made bad shots better by blowing them up, and made good photos precious by making them smaller. He always liked how I printed his pictures and usually agreed to my suggestions for cropping or printing them. Celebrities, buildings, fire hydrants, dogs and homeless people: Andy enjoyed taking pictures of anything.

The two of us were usually on the same page, sharing a vision influenced by the sexual and spiritual repression of our Catholic childhood. This shared vision served us both well. He was collaborating with an up-and-coming photographer and I enjoyed an association with a powerful, rich, iconic superstar artist, benefiting from his influence. It was a perfect marriage.

He took me and our cameras everywhere. During the late 1970s and early 1980s, the Swiss art dealers Bruno Bischofberger and Thomas Amman, along with the German art dealers Hans Meyer and Herman Wunche, revived Andy's career with numerous projects, and especially lots of what we called "Pay the Rent" portraits of rich industrialist's wives and families. It was during many of these trips that we really bonded. We would first take the Concorde to Paris, where we always ended up at Rue du Cherche-Midi, before traveling on to various points in Europe.

Andy and I both loved Dali, Man Ray, Marcel Duchamp and anything surreal. Andy is considered by some to be a late Dadaist. I kept this in mind as I thought about the right collaboration with him. The project was important to me and I did not want to waste the opportunity by producing just another portrait, which would be quickly forgotten or assigned to the genre of celebrity photojournalism. The famous photographs that Man Ray took of Marcel Duchamp in drag in 1921, *Rrose Sélavy,* were my inspiration. This was perfect, but how could we do something equally inspired without simply copying the brilliant idea that Man Ray and Duchamp had executed sixty years before? When is appropriation theft and inspiration creation?

Andy's Italian art dealer at the time, Luciano Anselmino, was also Man Ray's dealer, so I visited Man in Fregene, Italy. As a result of that visit, I was able to find my own voice and understood the project with Andy.

The Man Ray/Duchamp images were very dark, very moody, and very noir. My friend was very white and very bland. He had white skin and white hair; he was white right down to his soul. He was the whitest man I ever knew. It was clear that his pictures should be light, contrasting with the darkness of *Rrose Sélavy.*

Duchamp wore a woman's hat and dress, and Halston offered us a great sequined dress, but Andy and I declined. The whole drag thing was uncomfortable for both of us. We decided simply to change Andy's face and hair, but keep his signature jeans, white button down shirt, plaid tie and (during this period) cowboy boots. The tie and jeans would contrast with, and even lessen, the femininity of the wig and makeup.

We needed new hairpieces, and Andy knew just where to go: Jean Louis on 57th Street. Late one afternoon, after one of Andy's advertiser lunches and his workout with Lydia his trainer, we hopped into a taxi and headed uptown to the wig boutique. The owner himself, Jean Louis, showed us several hairpieces and escorted us into private rooms, where Andy tried them on. We had trouble deciding which was best, so he bought five different wigs that were used in the final shoots. It was amazing to realize how a new hairstyle—whether a man's hairpiece or a traditional woman's wig—could really "alter" one's image. This is where the phrase and the final concept for *Altered Images* originated—our visit to the 57th Street wiggery.

When we came to the shoots, the question arose of who would do the makeup. In the end, there were two shoots. For the first , we used the same makeup artist who made up the women in Andy's portrait commissions. In that shoot, my friend looks a bit haggard and peculiar, similar to some of the portraits Cindy Sherman takes of her collectors. This is because you really can't take a man and give him a woman's face with just a bit of makeup and clever facial expressions. This we learned. I have included those shots in this book because of their contextual importance, and also because, with time, all things become one, and the bad becomes good, and the good goes bad.

For the "glamour shoot," as I called it, we hired a theatrical makeup person, which really ratcheted it up a notch, finally turning him into a beauty. Some straight guys actually ask me if some of the shots of Andy were of Faye Dunaway! There were five wigs, two shoot days, sixteen contact sheets, and over three hundred different poses, of which a few are in this book.

In retrospect, the "demi-drag" was actually more like "the gender fuck" drag that was commonplace by the end of the 1980s. An example of this was the New York Dolls rock group, whose lead singer, David Johansen, dressed in jeans and women's high heels. Man dressed as woman or woman dressed as man? Pre-op or post-op? Mixed elements of style, traditional gender cues and mysterious sexuality—that's what we created, because we didn't know what else to do. It ended up being a glimpse into the future of blurred gender and alternative drag.

It is appropriate that a French publisher made this book project possible. I've always found that there is an understanding in

French culture of nuance and subtlety in photographic ideas, poses, facial expressions, body language, hand placement and other small details that differ slightly from one image to the other. That is so much of what fashion—an industry dominated by the French—is all about. Almost imperceptible change, visible only to those with the most discerning eye and the sharpest sensibility. Much of my work has been about nuance—seemingly slight differences that, when viewed by a perceptive eye, can provide a very different view of the subject.

Until now, the story behind the images, including the extent of Andy's participation and enthusiasm, has never really been told. The photos were taken in 1981. What follows is something that has taken twenty years to accomplish: the understanding of *Altered Images*.

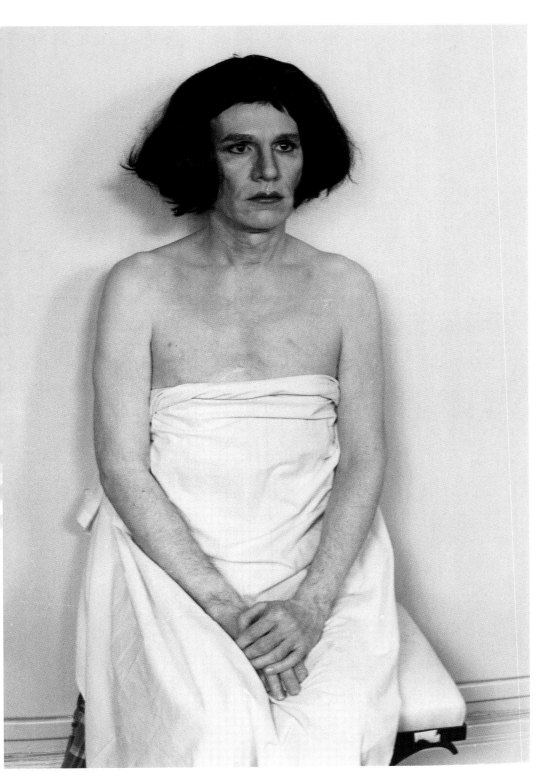

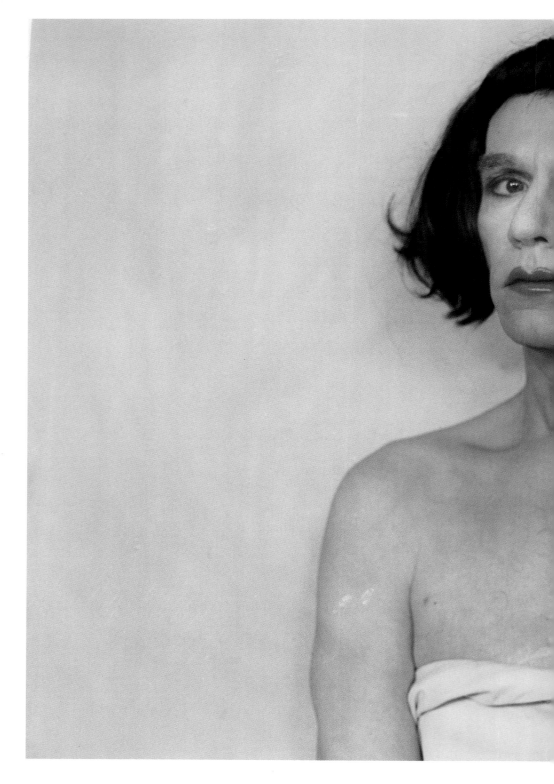

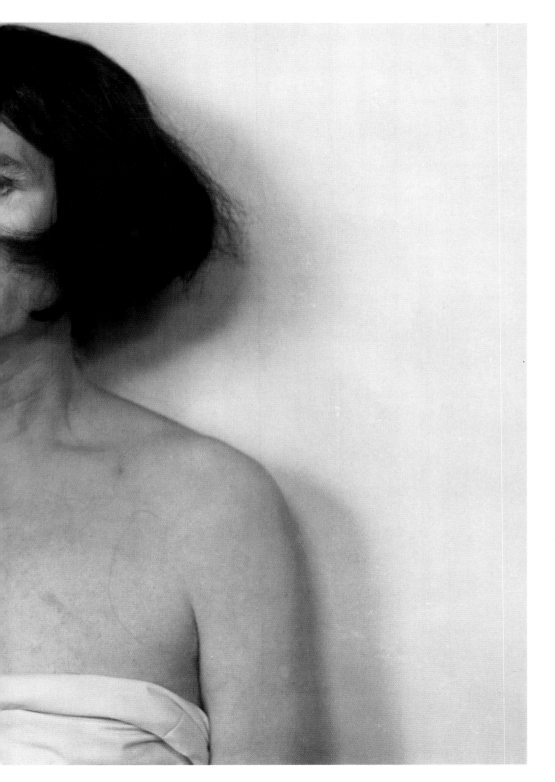

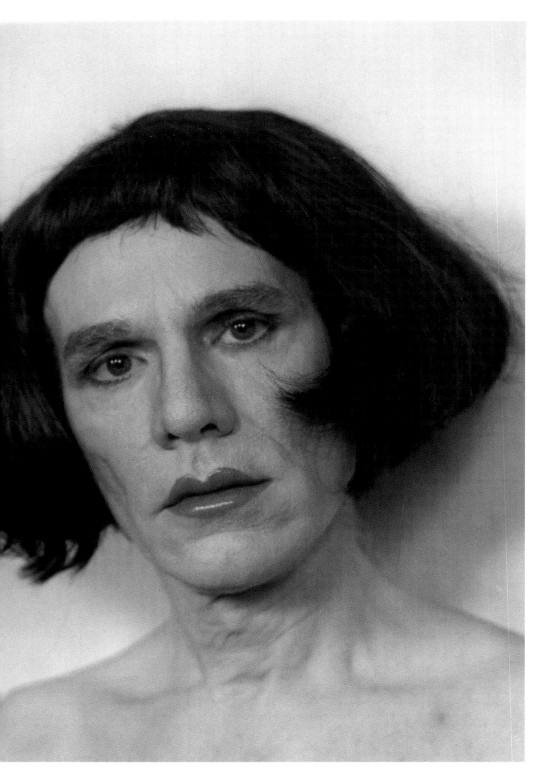

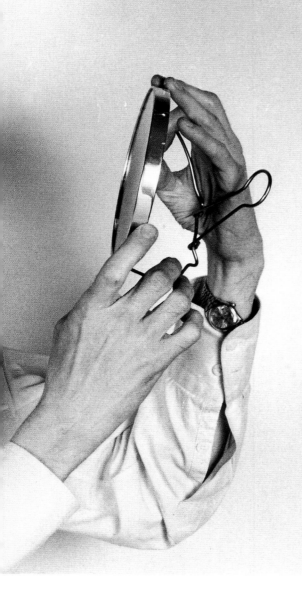

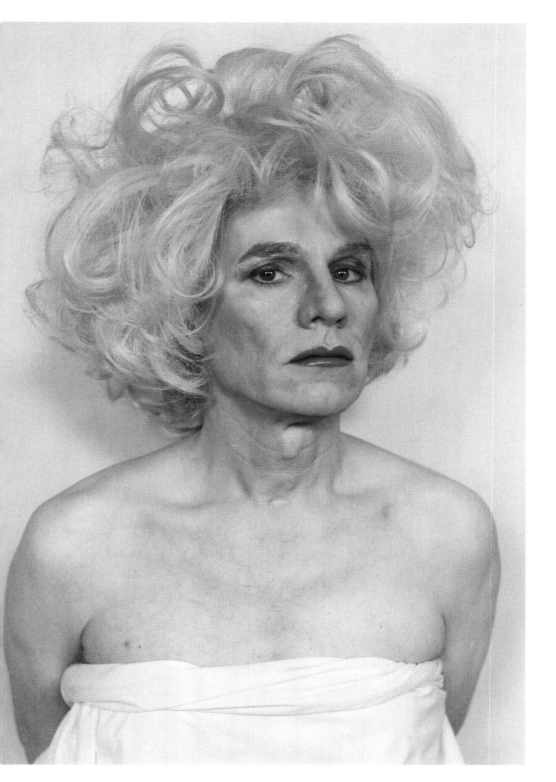

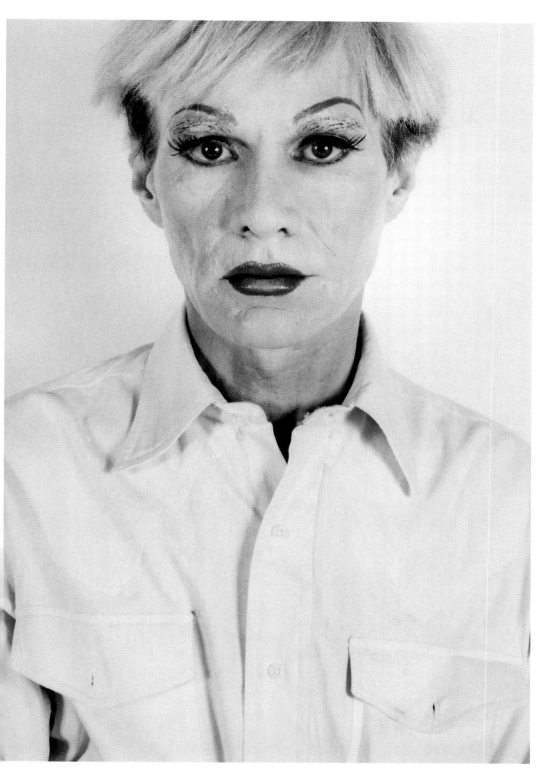

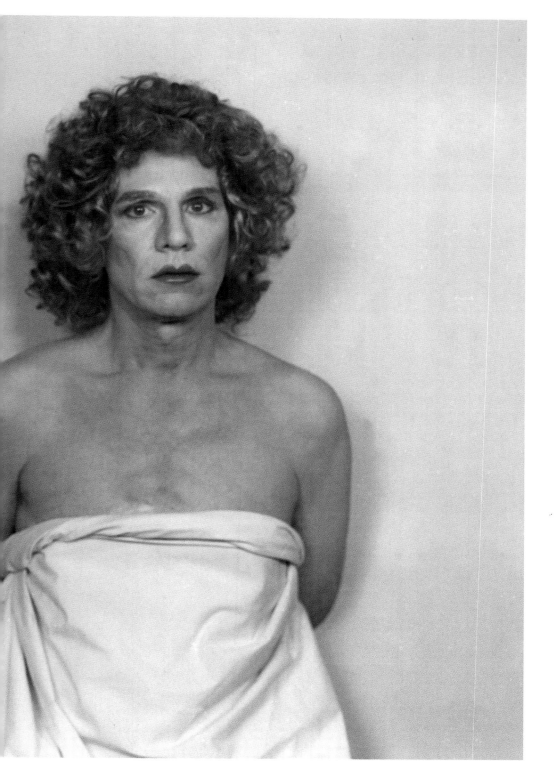

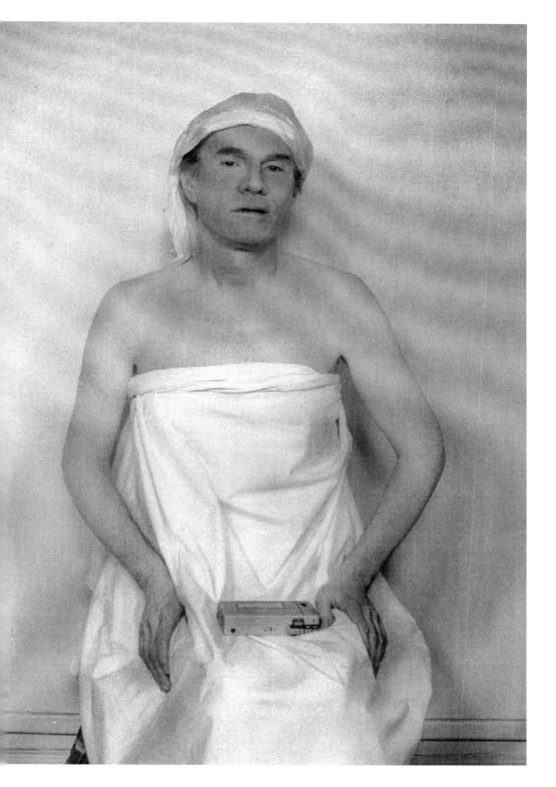

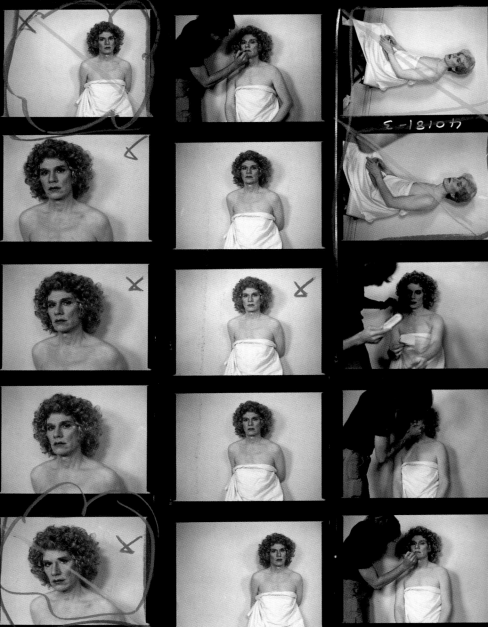

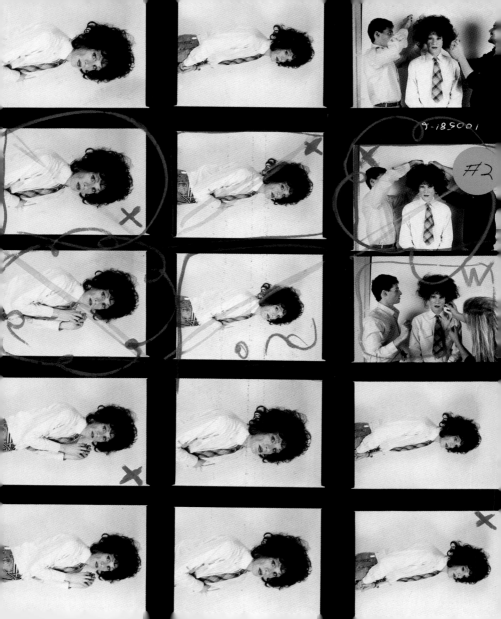

9-185001

#2

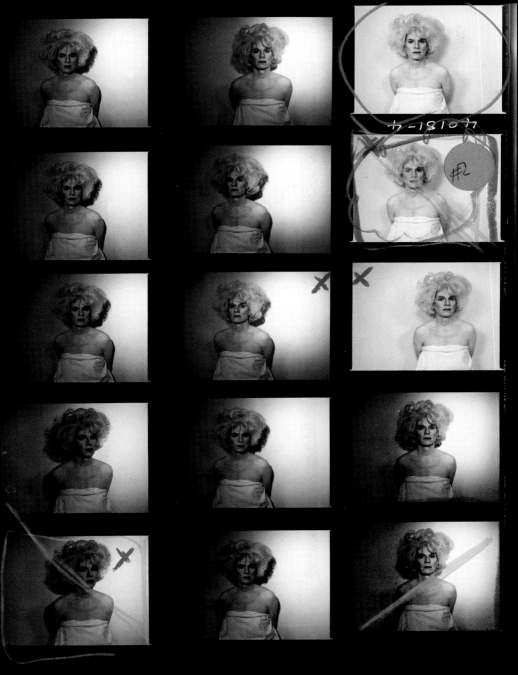

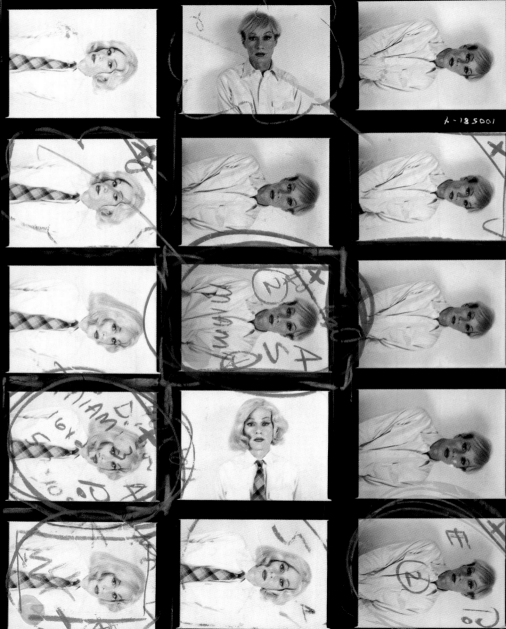

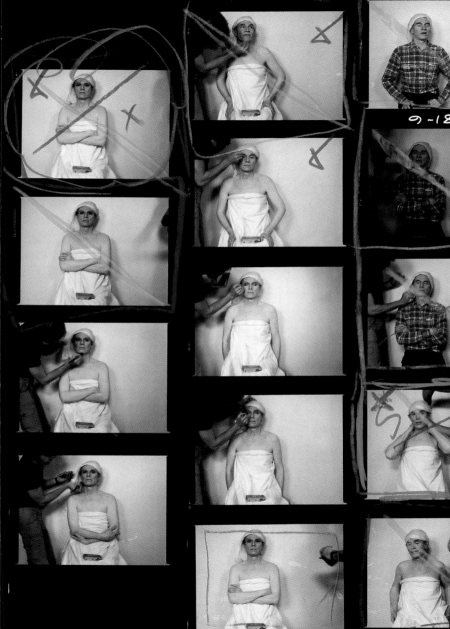

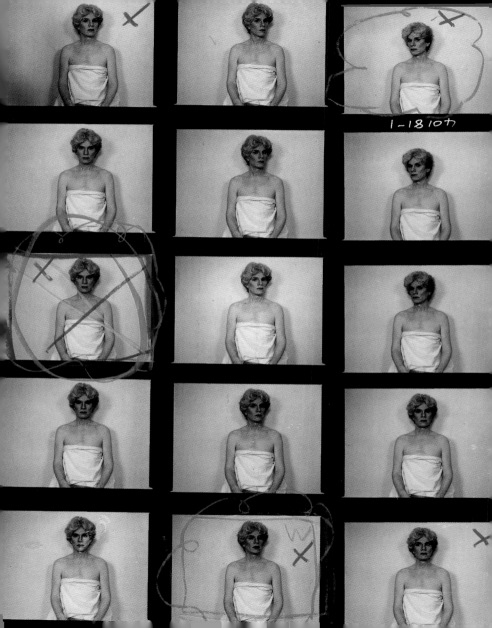

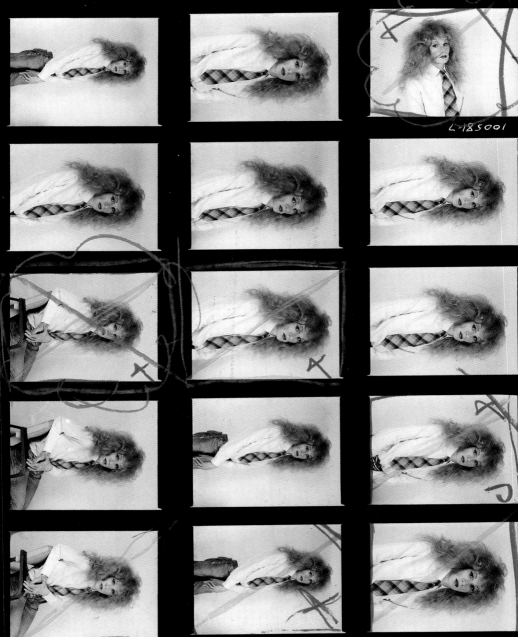

L-185001

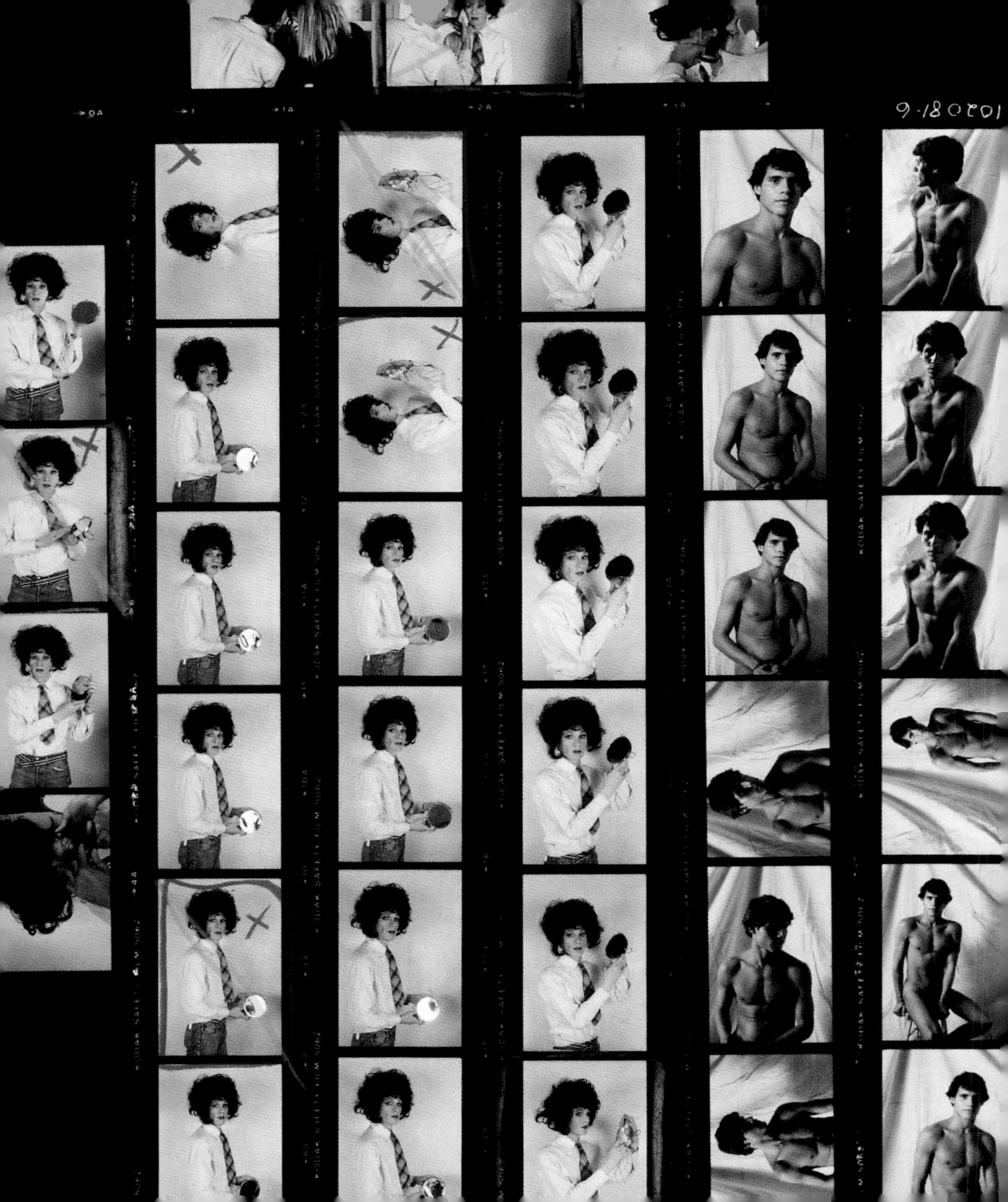

L-1810

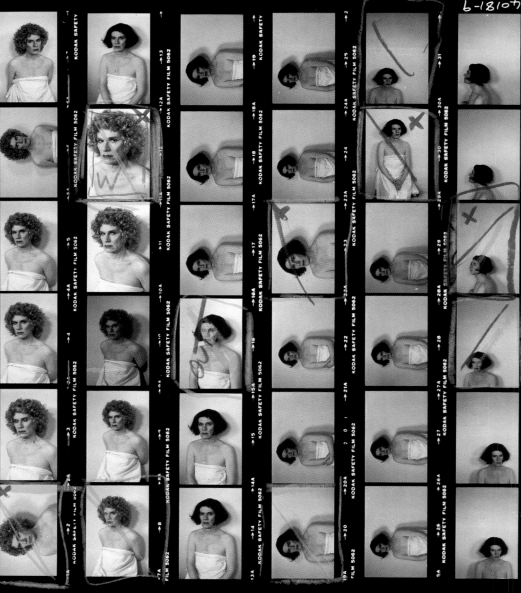

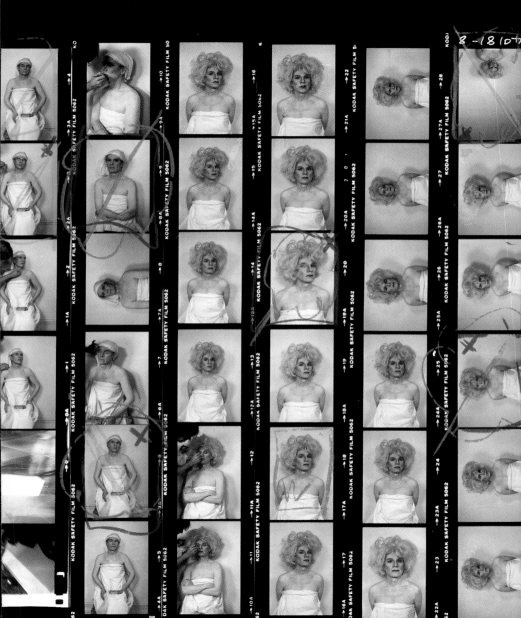

Christopher Makos's Exhibitions in 2001

Portraits of Warhol in Jeans, February 12, 2001, at Reina Sofia Gallery, Madrid, Spain.

Altered Images, portraits of Warhol, March 15, 2001, at JGM Gallery, Paris, France, premiering new book published by Assouline, pictures from the *Altered Images* series.

Art on Madison Avenue, May 3, 2001, at Kalvin Klein, New York, USA.

Photographs of Spain, 1983—2001, June 7, 2001, a retrospective at the Instituto Valenciano de Arte Moderno, Valencia, Spain.

Altered Images, photographs of Warhol, June 20, 2001, at the Contemporary Museum of Art of the City of Rome, Italy.

Photographs of Warhol in Germany (by Beuys, Boys, Makos and Warhol) and pictures from Makos's new Bruno Gummunder book, *Absolut Makos*, September 28, 2001, at Pictureshow Gallery, Berlin, Germany.

Acknowledgments

The author would like to thank Jean-Gabriel Mitterrand, Sean Strub and Peter Wise for the prints.